Eagle of the Sea

Kristin Bieber Domm
Illustrations by Jeffrey C. Domm

NIMBUS
PUBLISHING

Nimbus Publishing Limited
PO Box 9166
Halifax, NS   B3K 5M8
(902) 455-4286
nimbus.ca

Printed and bound in Canada
Design: Heather Bryan

Library and Archives Canada Cataloguing in Publication

Domm, Kristin Bieber
Eagle of the sea /
Kristin Bieber Domm ; illustrator, Jeffrey C. Domm.

ISBN 978-1-55109-749-7

1. Eagles—Juvenile literature. I. Domm, Jeffrey C., 1958- II. Title.

QL696.F32D64 2010   j598.9'42   C2009-907273-4

Canada   The Canada Council   Le Conseil des Arts   NOVA SCOTIA
          for the Arts   du Canada   Tourism, Culture and Heritage
We acknowledge the financial support of the Government of Canada through
the Book Publishing Industry Development Program (BPIDP) and the
Canada Council, and of the Province of Nova Scotia through the Department
of Tourism, Culture and Heritage for our publishing activities.

Acknowledgements

Bald eagles sometimes fly over our home in Cow Bay. They are likely the eagles that nest in the salt marsh nearby. The Cole Harbour Salt Marsh is an awe-inspiring landscape. We are grateful to Mary Osborne, David Kuhn, and all who have worked for the preservation of this important wetland habitat.

To the following people who contributed their particular expertise in the creation of this book, we express our sincere thanks: Luke, our skillful kayak guide; Doug Archibald and Peter MacDonald, wildlife biologists with the Nova Scotia Department of Natural Resources; the many students who offered feedback during Writers in the Schools visits; and the Nimbus team, for having eagle vision all along the way.

—Kristin & Jeff

I am a bald eagle.

My scientific name (*Haliaeetus leucocephalus*) means "white-headed sea eagle."

This name fits well because I live near the Atlantic Ocean and I grew white feathers on my head and tail when I was five years old and ready to find a mate.

(The word "bald" in my name means "marked with white.")

Now each spring my mate and I

fly cartwheels in the sky

and dive like roller coasters,

tumbling and whirling through the air

with our talons locked.

We do this high above
the Cole Harbour Salt Marsh—
the place where I was born,
the place where we built our nest
in a tall tree near the edge of the water.

When the tide goes out,
mudflats appear across the marsh.

When the tide comes in, a saltwater
lake ripples against the rocks.

Did you know that bald eagles build

the largest nest of any North American bird?

After the winter storms each year,

my mate and I fix up our nest,

adding branches and sticks to make

it strong, and cattails and moss

to make it soft inside.

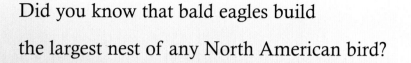

Because our nest is on a small peninsula, we can protect it.

Alert, we watch for predators across the marsh and over the forest treetops.

We also watch for food.

Sometimes eagles like me
are called "lions of the sky"
because we are skillful hunters.

We hunt by day for fish,
water birds, and small mammals.

Our powerful eyes can spot
prey from high up in the air.

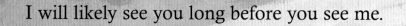

I will likely see you long before you see me.

(You are not the food I'm looking for,

but you might be a threat to my nest

so I will keep an eagle eye on you.)

My eyes are larger than yours—

and very strong.

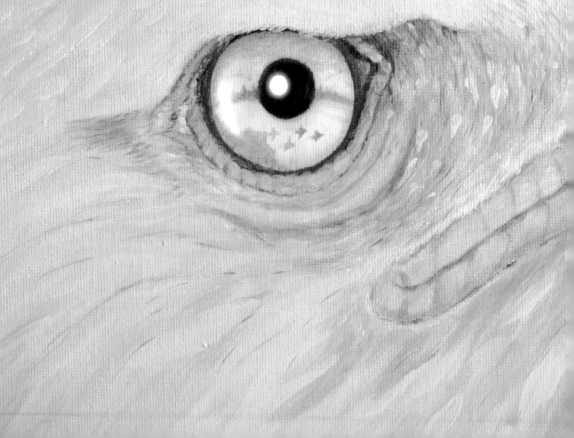

I see more colours than you do.

I can see farther distances, too.

Can *you* spot a duck or rabbit

from two kilometres away?

Flying is what I do best.

I glide on air currents, soaring for hours

with my huge wings open wide.

(They measure two metres from tip to tip.)

My feathers help me fly.

You might be surprised to know

I have seven thousand feathers.

My body feathers fit tightly together

to make me aerodynamic.

I use my tail feathers to steer and the flight feathers

on my wings to speed up or slow down.

I carefully arrange and clean my feathers

to keep them smooth for flying

and I waterproof them with a special oil

released near the base of my tail.

I need waterproof feathers for fishing.

Sometimes, if the fish I catch

is too heavy to fly with,

I hold it in my talons and swim to shore.

This spring I laid two large, white eggs.

My mate and I have kept them warm
and safe from predators for the past five weeks.

Today, inside one of the eggs,
I can feel something moving
and pecking at the shell.

Our eaglet (that's what baby eagles are called)
will use an egg tooth—
a bump on its beak that falls off later—
to peck its way out.

It's hard work.

Here's our first eaglet, covered

in fluffy, light grey down.

Its half-open eyes are brown.

And its legs are pink.

In a few weeks its legs will turn yellow

and its soft down will darken.

Later our eaglet will grow feathers.

Now both eaglets have hatched.

For a month I will keep these eaglets
warm and dry and safe in the nest
while my mate brings back food.
(Sometimes we'll switch jobs.)

We will have to be careful
not to hurt them with our
sharp talons.

Our eaglets will learn many things, like
how to take care of their feathers and
how to tear up food into bits.

In time their legs will grow
sturdy and their wings
will grow strong.

Soon they'll be ready to learn to fly.

By the time these eaglets are ten weeks old,

they will have flight feathers,

and we will have to dare them

to leave the nest, to try their wings,

to begin searching for food on their own.

By the end of summer, they will know

how to take care of themselves,

and then they will have to leave us

to survive on their own.

In the winter

eagles like me often meet in groups

to hunt and eat together.

This helps the youngest eagles survive.

It also helps them find mates later on.

Sometimes in winter

I join bald eagles gathering

in other parts of Nova Scotia.

But I always return

to the Cole Harbour Salt Marsh—

an excellent homeland

for an eagle of the sea like me.

More About Bald Eagles

Bald eagles live here in North America—and nowhere else on earth. They are Canada's largest raptors. Adult bald eagles stand about seventy-six centimetres tall and can weigh up to seven kilograms. Although they look much the same, females are usually slightly larger and heavier than males. Bald eagles have a large curved beak and huge feet (three toes in front, one in the back) with sharp talons. Their eyes are protected by a bony eyebrow ridge (which gives them a serious look) and by a clear eyelid that closes from side to side. Besides having a keen sense of sight, bald eagles also hear well. But they don't have a keen sense of smell or taste—helpful for scavengers like eagles, who sometimes eat things that are not too savoury.

Bald eagles can fly up to three kilometres above the earth and can dive at speeds of 160 kilometres per hour. They produce a high-pitched call that carries long distances. Bald eagles defend their breeding range (a one- to two-square-kilometre area where they nest) but not their home range (a ten- to fifteen-square-kilometre area where they hunt and scavenge for food).

Bald eagles generally mate for life, but if one mate dies, the other will choose a new mate. Bald eagles in captivity can live up to fifty years. In the wild, their lifespan is much shorter. They are vulnerable to disease and starvation, especially when young, and their habitat is often impacted by human activity. In many parts of North America, bald eagles are still struggling to survive.

But in Nova Scotia bald eagles are thriving. They are breeding in increasing numbers all across the province. Protected by the Wildlife Act since 1987, bald eagles have also benefited from habitat conservation and supplemental winter feeding programs. They are most easily spotted at winter gathering places where food is plentiful, such as near the Pictou Causeway, along the Shubenacadie River, and in the Annapolis Valley.

For the past thirty years Annapolis Valley poultry farmers have placed chicken out on the snow to supplement the winter diet of bald eagles. This has helped young eagles survive and adult eagles stay strong and healthy for the breeding season. Each January in the town of Sheffield Mills, Eagle Watch Weekend celebrates this huge winter gathering of bald eagles.

Habitat conservation in Nova Scotia has also helped bald eagles thrive. The Cole Harbour Salt Marsh was donated to the province in 1998 by Mary Osborne and David Kuhn, working in cooperation with the Nature Conservancy of Canada. This salt marsh on the eastern shore is home to at least one nesting pair of bald eagles. Also known as the Peter McNab Kuhn Conservation Area, this 930-hectare wetland habitat is an important ecosystem for migratory waterfowl, a key element in the eagle diet. Habitat conservation such as this is crucial to the survival of many species—including the bald eagle.

Websites to Explore: www.eaglens.ca
www.handcockwildlife.org; www.hww.ca